To: Brecque

From: Dad & Marcia

some good
things to think
about en here!

Book Design: Brian Frantz

Finish Strong is a registered trademark of Finish Strong LLC. and used under license.

Simple Truths is a registered trademark.
Printed and bound in the United States of America

ISBN 978-1-60810-142-9

800-900-3427
www.simpletruths.com

01-WOZ 11

Photo Credits :

Cover : Shutterstock

Dedication Page : Thinkstock

Introduction : Shutterstock

Thinkstock : 6,10,12,16,30,34,36,48,55,64,78,94,96,112,117,124,127,139,144,151

Shutterstock : 18,24,40,42,46,60,67,72,76,83,84,88,100,102,106,108,114,120,131,132,136,142,148,154

Mary Anderson : 28

Brian Frantz : 70

Fotolia : 52

FINISH STRONG

Motivational Quotes...to help you go the distance

By Dan Green

Introduction

Finish Strong!

**Those are two words that can create
a powerful attitude for achievement in life,
sport and business.**

Since the release of my book, *Finish Strong*, in 2008, I've heard from
thousands of people across the globe who've expressed their excitement
about adopting the *"Finish Strong"* attitude...one which has helped them
overcome adversity and capitalize on opportunity. A *"Finish Strong"*
attitude is applicable for everyone—teachers, students, athletes,
business professionals, parents, doctors, patients, sales teams,
professional sport teams (thank you New Orleans), churches
and many more.

As an extension of
the "*Finish Strong*"
attitude, *Finish Strong*
Motivational Quotes exists
to help you reinforce the core
values of the "*Finish Strong*"
attitude and energize you to action.

It is my hope that you will find strength, inspiration and
motivation within the pages that follow. Keep it close by,
refer to it often and always choose to *Finish Strong!*

Energy and persistence alter all things.

Benjamin Franklin

FINISH STRONG. 7

A person who never made a mistake
never tried anything new.

Albert Einstein

We don't see things as they are,

we see things as we are.

Anais Nin

Chance favors those in motion.

James H. Austin

FINISH STRONG

Life is **10 percent** what you make it and **90 percent** how you take it.

Irving Berlin

$\mathcal{T}$he will to do springs from the

knowledge that we can do.

James Allen

*T*he most powerful weapon on earth

is the **human soul** on fire.

Ferdinand Foch

Chop your own wood
and it will warm you twice.

Henry Ford

For some the day is over,

for others it's just beginning.

Unknown

Decide what you **want**,

decide what you are **willing** to exchange for it.

Establish your **priorities** and go to work.

H.L. Hunt

Let me tell you the secret

that has led me to my goal.

My strength lies solely in my tenacity.

Louis Pasteur

$\mathcal{Y}$ou have to expect things of yourself
before you can do them.

Michael Jordan

FINISH STRONG® 23

$\mathcal{D}$on't be afraid to take a big step

if one is indicated.

You can't cross a chasm

in two small jumps.

David Lloyd George

Regardless of what came before or what has yet to come, what's important at this moment in time is how you choose to respond to the event. Will you fight? Or will you lie down? The choice is yours.

Always choose to Finish Strong.

Dan Green

How you **respond to the challenge** in the second half will determine what you become after the game, whether you are a winner or a loser.

Lou Holtz

The only thing that stands
between a person
and what they want in life
is the will to try it and the faith
to **believe** it possible.

Rich DeVos

$\mathcal{T}$he only thing even in this world are the number of hours in a day.
The difference in winning and losing is **what you do with those hours**.

Woody Hayes

*T*he road to success
has no **speed limit**.

L. Nicole Green

*K*eep coming back, and though the world
may romp across your spine, let every game's end
find you still upon the battling line; for when the
One Great Scorer comes to mark against your name,
he writes—not that you won or lost—
but how you played the game.

Grantland Rice

FINISH STRONG

It doesn't matter
where you've been,
it only matters
where you are **going**.

Brian Tracy

A man can be as great as he wants to be.
If you believe in yourself and have the courage,
the determination, the dedication, the competitive
drive and if you are willing to sacrifice the little
things in life and pay the price for the things that
are worthwhile, it can be done. Once a man has
made a commitment to a way of life, he puts the
greatest strength in the world behind him.
It's something we call "heart power".
Once a man has made this commitment,
nothing will stop him short of success.

Vince Lombardi

If you realized how powerful your thoughts are, you would never think a negative thought.

Peace Pilgrim

FINISH STRONG

Feed your faith
and doubt will **starve**
to death.

Unknown

You are never a loser until you quit trying.

Mike Ditka

Have the dogged determination to follow through to achieve your goal;

regardless of circumstances or whatever other people say, think or do.

Paul J. Meyer

*T*he difference between winning and losing is most often ... not quitting.

Walt Disney

46

FINISH STRONG

*D*iscipline is the bridge between

goals and accomplishments.

Jim Rohn

When you have to make a choice
and don't make it,
that is in itself a **choice**.

William James

If you're going through hell,

keep going.

Winston Churchill

Your reason and passion are the rudder and the sails of your seafaring soul. If either your sails or your rudder be broken, you can but toss and drift, or else be held at a standstill in mid-seas. For reason, ruling alone, is a force confining; and passion, unattended, is a flame that burns to its own destruction.

Kahlil Gibran

FINISH STRONG. 53

The person on top of the mountain

did not fall there.

Unknown

Desire is the starting point of all achievement, not a hope, not a wish, but a keen pulsating desire which transcends everything.

Napoleon Hill

Show me a guy

who's afraid to look bad,
and I'll show you a guy
you can beat every time.

Lou Brock

Many of life's failures are people who did not realize how close they were to success when they gave up.

Thomas Edison

FINISH STRONG

$\mathcal{N}$othing will work

unless you do.

John Wooden

$\mathcal{E}$very day is another new day of our lives. Think not of what you did yesterday, but what you can do for yourself today. Don't be known as one that could have or should have, but as one that did.

Jerry Pate

The last of one's freedoms is to choose one's attitude in any given circumstance.

Viktor Frankl

We could hardly wait
to get up in the morning.

Wilbur Wright

Set your course
by the stars,
not by the lights
of every passing ship.

General Omar N. Bradley

FINISH STRONG. 67

*C*hange your thoughts
and you change your world.

Norman Vincent Peale

The only thing we have to fear is fear itself.

Franklin D. Roosevelt

The fire which **enlightens**
is the same fire
which **consumes**.

Henri Frederic Amiel

FINISH STRONG.

*C*ourage ... it's fear holding on

a minute longer.

General George S. Patton

FINISH STRONG.

*A*ny time you try to **win** everything, you must be willing to **lose** everything.

Larry Csonka

You can't change the past,

and you can't predict the future,

but you can ruin the present

by worrying about both.

Unknown

*H*ave the **courage to live**.
Anyone can die.

Robert Cody

$\mathcal{D}$ig the well **before** you are thirsty.

Chinese Proverb

Do or do not ...

there is no try!

George Lucas

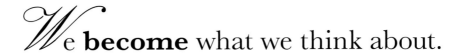

We **become** what we think about.

Earl Nightingale

$\mathscr{T}$o get what
you've never had;
you must do
what you've never done.

Unknown

FINISH STRONG.

*T*he bad news is *time flies.*

The good news is **you're the pilot**.

Michael Altshuler

I am a great believer in luck,
and I find that the harder I work,
the more I have of it.

Thomas Jefferson

In any moment of decision,
the best thing you can do is the **right** thing,
the next best thing is the **wrong** thing
and the worst thing you can do is **nothing**.

Theodore Roosevelt

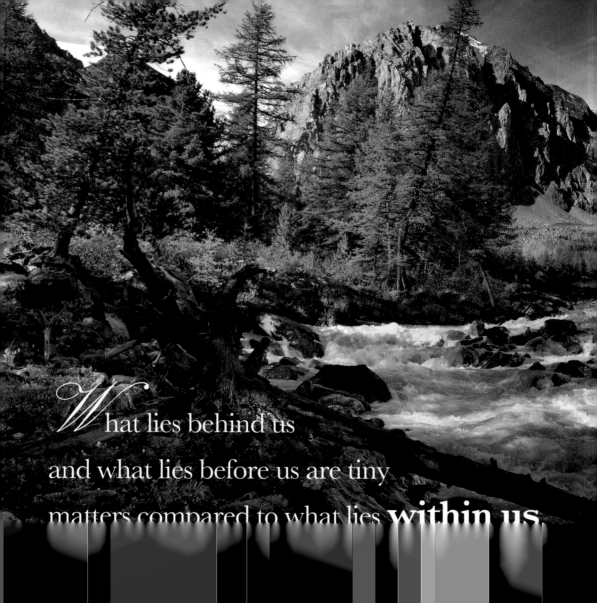

What lies behind us and what lies before us are tiny matters compared to what lies **within us**.

FINISH STRONG

A word of encouragement
during a failure is worth more
than an hour of praise after success.

Unknown

Passion is the genesis of genius.

Anthony Robbins

It's not what happens to you that matters,

*it's how **you choose** to respond that does.*

Dan Green

It doesn't matter what you drive as long as you're on the **right track**.

Kathryn Green

FINISH STRONG

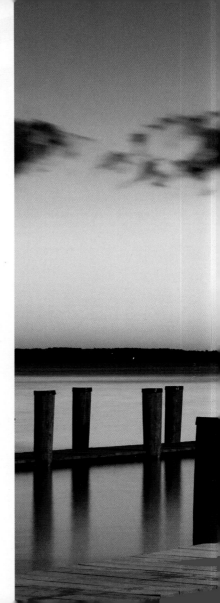

It's never too late

to be what

you might have been.

George Eliot

FINISH STRONG. 97

$\mathcal{L}$ife takes on meaning when you become **motivated**, **set goals** and **charge after them** in an unstoppable manner.

Les Brown

*D*estiny is no matter of **chance**.

It is a matter of **choice**.

It is not a thing to be **waited for**,

it is a thing to be **achieved**.

William Jennings Bryan

Nothing happens unless first a dream.

Carl Sandburg

FINISH STRONG.

Keep on going,

and the chances are that **you will stumble**

on something, perhaps when you are least

expecting it. I never heard of anyone ever

stumbling on something sitting down.

Charles Kettering

*C*ourage is almost a contradiction in terms.
It means a strong desire to live
taking the form of a readiness to die.

Gilbert K. Chesterton

$\mathcal{T}$here is a time to let things happen
and a time to make things happen.

Hugh Prather

Effort only fully releases its reward after a person refuses to quit.

Napoleon Hill

FINISH STRONG

107

*O*nly those who will **risk** going too far

can possibly find out

how far **they can go**.

T.S. Eliot

*T*he difference between a successful person and others is not the lack of **strength**, not a lack of **knowledge**, but rather a **lack of will**.

Vince Lombardi

$\mathcal{P}$lay the game for more

than you can afford to lose ...

only then will you learn the game.

Winston Churchill

$\mathcal{G}$reat **beginnings**
are not as important
as the way one **finishes**.

Dr. James Dobson

Even if you're on the right track,
you'll get **run over** if you just sit there.

Will Rogers

*T*o accomplish great things,

we must not only **act**,

but also **dream**;

not only **plan**,

but also **believe**.

Anatole France

FINISH STRONG

*G*reat minds have purposes,

others have wishes.

Washington Irving

We **confide** in our strength,

without boasting of it;

we **respect** that of others,

without fearing it.

Thomas Jefferson

$\mathcal{I}$n the long run,

you hit only what you aim at.

Henry David Thoreau

What it lies in our power to do,
it lies in our power not to do.

Aristotle

*I*mperfect action is better than perfect inaction.

Harry Truman

*N*othing changes until something moves.

Albert Einstein

FINISH STRONG

125

*S*ometimes we stare
so long at a door
that is closing
that we see too late
the one that is open.

Alexander Graham Bell

We are all faced with a series of great opportunities brilliantly disguised as impossible situations.

Charles R. Swindoll

$\mathcal{D}$o what you love.
Know your own **bone**;
gnaw at it,
bury it,
unearth it,
and gnaw it still.

Henry David Thoreau

$\mathcal{D}$o what you **love**...

All things are possible to him who believes.

Mark 9:23 NASB

FINISH STRONG.

The cost of regret

far exceeds the price of discipline.

Peter Lowe

Strength does not come

from physical capacity,

it comes from an indomitable will.

Mahatma Gandhi

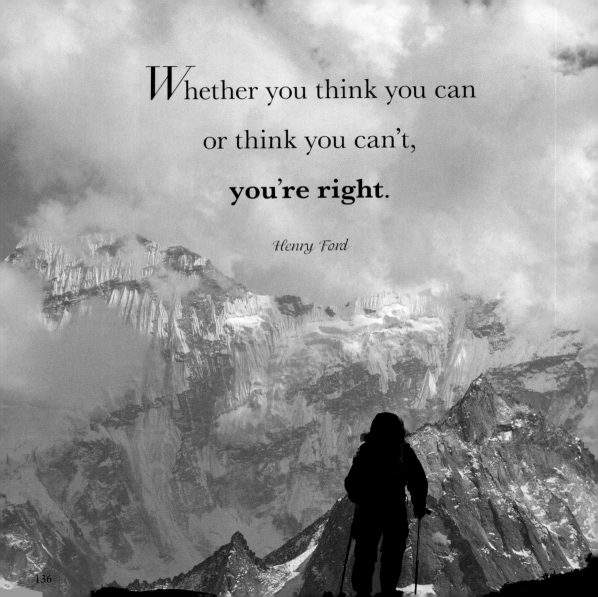

Whether you think you can
or think you can't,
you're right.

Henry Ford

FINISH STRONG

$\mathcal{P}$eople who take risks

are the people you'll lose against.

John Sculley

FINISH STRONG

Vision without action is a daydream.

Action without vision is a nightmare.

Japanese Proverb

*M*ost of us have **far more courage**

than we ever dreamed we possessed.

Dale Carnegie

*Y*our attitude, not your aptitude, will determine your altitude.

Zig Ziglar

The secret to success
is consistency
of purpose.

Benjamin Disraeli

The he will to win is not nearly

as important as **the will to prepare**.

Bobby Knight

*C*ircumstances are beyond human control,

but **our conduct** is in our own power.

Benjamin Disraeli

$\mathcal{T}$here is only one way to succeed

in anything and that is

to give it everything.

Vince Lombardi

The trouble
with not having a goal
is that you can spend your life
running up and down the field
and never score!

Bill Copeland

I have fought the good fight.
I have finished the race,
I have kept the faith.

2 Timothy 4:7 NIV

FINISH STRONG.

*I*t's not where you start—

it's **where you finish** that counts.

Zig Ziglar

FINISH STRONG®

ABOUT THE AUTHOR

Dan Green is an entrepreneur with a passion for finishing strong in everything he does. Over the past 20 years, he has excelled in business and life in large part to his adoption of the "Finish Strong" attitude. He currently serves as Executive Vice President and partner with Simple Truths and is also the founder of Finish Strong, LLC.

Dan is the author of three inspirational books; *Finish Strong, Finish Strong Teen Athlete* and *Finish Strong Motivational Quotes*. The first *Finish Strong* book was used by Drew Brees and the New Orleans Saints as a guiding theme during the 2009 season and ultimately their first Super Bowl victory.

In 1996, Dan trademarked the words "Finish Strong" with the intent to inspire the world. Since that time, he has been the evangelist for spreading its powerful message to individuals across the globe. As a result, thousands of people from all walks of life have made a positive change in their life by embracing the Finish Strong attitude as their own personal platform for achievement—in life, sport and business.

Dan lives outside of Chicago, is married and the father of two amazing girls. He enjoys playing the guitar, golfing, boxing, fitness and motorsports.

For more information about Dan, to inquire about speaking engagements, or to learn more about incorporating Finish Strong into your next event, visit www.FinishStrong.com or send an email to ContactDan@finishstrong.com.

www.finishstrong.com

simple truths®
Motivational & Inspirational Gifts

If you have enjoyed this book, we invite you to check out our entire collection of gift books, with free inspirational movies, at **www.simpletruths.com**.

You'll discover it's a great way to inspire friends and family, or to thank your best customers and employees.

For more information, please visit us at:

www.simpletruths.com

or call us toll free …

800-900-3427